I0503613

THE
SUPER-HIGHWAY
OF RELEVANCY

GETTING MORE PEOPLE TO CHOOSE
YOUR BRAND, MORE OFTEN, INDEFINITELY

ANNE CANDIDO

Copyright 2019 by Anne Candido.
All Rights Reserved

ISBN: 9781705378199

Cover Art: Richard Candido

DEDICATION

*For my mom, my grandma and all the women
who have come before trailblazing the path
and showing women the way.*

TABLE OF CONTENTS

GLOSSARY OF TERMS

For the sake of readability, I have made the following simplifications:

- "Start-up" has two definitions. It is what we call businesses in the early stages of their journey. But, it is also a proxy for the entrepreneurial mentality associated with starting something new. Though this book references more of the former, it is relevant for any size business from small to large because of the latter. Launching a new product, re-sparking your brand or penetrating a new customer demographic will all necessitate a start-up mentality. Your team may look slightly different, but the entrepreneurial start-up spirit will be the key to unlocking new growth.

- I use "Product" as a proxy for the tangible offering or service that defines a business. It is important to note that a service and even a person or people can be a brand. Consider Fed-Ex, LeBron James and The Beatles as examples here. Brand-Love is essential for all of these brands to grow.

- I use "Customer" to define anyone buying products or services from your business. Some call this a "Consumer", but I didn't want to alienate those of you whose primary target is a B2B (business-to-business) client. These relationships benefit from Brand-Love as well.

MISSION STATEMENT

My vision in writing this *Brand-Building Handbook* is to serve as a compass for those of you contemplating or already in the throes of a start-up or small business. But I found as I started to socialize this vision with these entrepreneurial warriors that I had over-looked a very obvious point of explanation — what really is brand-building?

Many have heard of "brand-management", which most associate with the marketing of a brand and the act of making television commercials, developing digital content, managing social channels, and conducting public relations and promotions. Though a simplified role description, this is for the most part true. But building a brand starts *way* before any actual marketing activation -- or at least it should. Brand building in its most fundamental form is the strategy, i.e. the means and methods, for increasing your brand's value. The objective is to stimulate short-term revenue generation, which translates into the bigger prize of long-term sustainable growth.

Inherently, this requires more people to choose your brand, more often, indefinitely. This is what is referred to in a profit-and-loss statement (P&L) as top-line growth. However, when trying to improve profit, many start-ups tend to defer focus on top-line growth and instead concentrate on levers they feel are more in their control like reducing cost of goods or expenses. What they fail to realize is often times these factors are contingent on driving the top-line as well. For example, you can't scale-up to increase your order quantity and reduce the cost per unit unless there is demand. And you can't drive demand (aka more people choosing your brand more often) unless you have enough personal and identifiable value to stimulate it.

Most entrepreneurs will initially try to generate demand by building value around a problem/solution proposition. This might be very effective...until someone generates a "good enough" knock-off and undercuts your price. Those who persevere and enjoy sustainable growth have a built-in fortifier protecting them from these brutal attacks. Some may call it "trust" or "reliability" or "familiarity" or a multitude of other emotional descriptors, but what it all boils down to is...love. **Customers unequivocally and pervasively profess their love of your brand through their repeated testimony and purchase.** To achieve this, you must be intentional in how you build your brand. Which is the inspiration for this *Brand-Building Handbook*.

As a *Handbook* implies, you will find it to the point, as well as dense. I did this to make it actionable. **If you find yourself struggling with putting any of it into practice, contact me. I would be happy to be your guide.**

And with that, let's get it started.

CHAPTER 1

OF ALL THE THINGS TO WORRY ABOUT, WHY BUILDING BRAND-LOVE?

Building and working with start-ups can be intoxicating because there is so much energy that comes with blazing new trails, following your passions and creating something novel that customers will appreciate. These forward thinkers are also the lifeblood of our economy since they create industry bringing in new jobs and stimulating competition. This keeps a business' focus and pulse on innovation and what's best for those buying their products and services.

Then why do 50% of new businesses fail in the first 5 years[1]? Simple, they never learned how to translate their product into a brand. **The difference between a product and a brand is probably the most over-looked yet mission-critical nuance for exponential business growth.** And customers falling in love with your brand is the key to making that transition. Why? Because more than 90% of decision-making is based on emotion[2]. **Yes, it's heart-led NOT brain-led.** Brand builders who understand this and intentionally choose to cultivate Brand-Love persevere.

Let's take Nike for example: Their slogan for decades has been "Just do It", a call-to-action for everyone to rise above their excuses and unleash their inner athlete. They action this slogan by creating hyper-relevant ways of connecting with potential customers, creating an ecosystem surrounding them at every touch-point. These aspiring athletes become exposed to the brand through concept stores, training tools, as well as entertainment and pop-culture integrations (Who remembers *Space Jam?*). The brand has spurned fashion movements where Sneaker-Heads rule and emblazon power in sports teams who don the iconic swoosh on their uniforms and a silhouette of a man soaring for a dunk on their shoes. Then there are the endorsers, the likes of Kevin Hart and Serena Williams who embody the brand's equity in mind, body and spirit and become inspirational role-models. All of these intricately woven interactions create a ripple effect leading to a stronger affinity for the brand, an ethos of enamored brand lovers which steam-rolls the competition. This is the key to Nike's domination of the athletic shoe and apparel industry. Shoes and apparel may be basic commodities in the everyday world, but in Nike's world, they are coveted treasures. We will talk more in Chapter 2 on how staying a commodity can be the death of your business.

Now don't get me wrong. It is imperative your product deliver on the promised performance criteria to meet your customer's needs and wants, but it is not enough anymore to just be good or even the best. This is the price of entry. Which is why Nike and other thriving brands don't rely on claims of functional dominancy (i.e. I am the best performing basketball shoe) to win. Instead, they exemplify their dominance through emotionally rich offerings (i.e. Jordan's and LeBron's). In this world of saturated consumerism, you need to hardwire your brand to your customer in unexpected yet authentic ways. You must trigger an irrational affinity for it and only it in order to differentiate and rise above the noise of competition or what is worse...pure 'ol complacency. **In other words, driving exponential brand growth means ensuring your product hitches a ride onto your customers' hearts and souls as well as their minds.**

Don't let the intoxicating nature of your start-up lull you into believing that you have created an offering so unique there is no competition. EVERYONE has competition. Even apathy is competition. Somehow, people have been getting by a long time without you. Those "workarounds" are your competition and must be acknowledged and embraced to effectively and efficiently grow Brand-Love. Understanding your competition will help you clarify who you are, who you want to be and your point of differentiation. Armed with this knowledge, you can build essential emotional connections.

Think of it this way: Every product that is born needs to traverse a path in order to get to the customer. In traditional brand-building, this is called the "Path to Purchase". But actually, there are ALWAYS multiple paths. Think of it more like an intertwined network of highways that provide multiple routes for reaching your customer destination. And just as in reality, the quickest route may not necessarily be the shortest distance. The speed in reaching your customer can be impacted by the infrastructure of the highway itself, the vehicle you are traveling in, your driving conditions and those on the highway getting in your way. For example, you may have what you believe to be a short highway with the cheapest price. But if all your competition is also traveling on this highway, what happens? Traffic jam! Who wins in this case? The ones who eek out some margins to get their meager scraps from retailers. All others find themselves running out of gas (aka cash) and must take the exit ramp to "Irrelevancy and Broken Dreams".

On the flip side, you can build your own personal highway that bypasses the jam on "Interstate Cheap Price/Commodity". This does take effort, time and may be longer. But since it is only you and your unique emotional connections with your customer that traverse this highway, your chances of reaching her significantly increase. **This is your "Super-Highway of Relevancy"**. If I also promised the potential reward is much greater on this highway, is there any doubt which one you should be on?

And let me just acknowledge that, yes, it is harder to build your own Super-Highway, which is why big companies (referred to as BigCo's) do have big teams, big budgets and big agencies devoted to building one. But, here is a secret...it is not the amount of money and people that matters. It is the *quality* of thinking uncovering high-potential customer insights that will allow your brand to uniquely yet authentically connect to their heart, soul and mind. This next-level thinking can be accomplished with the right guidance from this book and later with additional consultation from me. Unfortunately, this means, depending on where you are on your journey, you may need to undo some of the branding decisions you have already made. Directional change might be hard especially since so much critical capital and time have been invested in getting where you are. If you struggle to let go, this process is going to be very painful when it comes, and it must come. Instead, embrace the philosophy of Mark Zuckerberg and "Move fast and break things" because your customer is waiting for YOU. Building your "Super-Highway of Relevancy" takes construction, demolition, messiness and courage. And, you will only know what will work by doing, winning as well as failing and redoing. So, let's get started.

CHAPTER 2

DO YOU HAVE A BRAND OR JUST A PRODUCT?

I would venture to guess that 95% of you probably read this chapter title and said, "Huh? What does she mean? I have a name, this thing people are buying, I even market on social media. Of course I have a brand. And, why does it matter anyway if I am making money?" In order to get to why it matters, we must first probe into this fundamental question: what are you really selling?

Consider the popular product of sandwich cookies. There is a wide range to choose from all doing the same job of satisfying your sweet tooth. But there is one favorite always rising to the top -- the prototypical sandwich cookie empire of Oreo. So, how does Mondelez sell 40 billion Oreo cookies a year to the tune of $2 billion in global annual revenue?[3] Not on taste alone. Arguably, in a blind taste test, you may not even detect a difference between an Oreo and its nearest competitor. They generate the revenue only because Mondelez isn't selling just a cookie. They are selling the euphoria of a dessert.

Think about it...the entire ritual of eating an Oreo - TWIST, LICK, DUNK - has been celebrated for over 100 years. The company adds a variety of seasonal flavors to commemorate holidays and special occasions enticing you to experiment (Apple Pie Oreos, anyone?). All of this is fueled by campaigns that creatively intertwine this dessert cookie into life's best moments. Consider its

2013 "Wonderfilled" animated marketing campaign suggesting that sharing an Oreo "can bring about a positive change in perspective," according to Janda Lukin, then Director, Oreo at Mondelez International, Inc. Or, most recently in 2017, the "Oreo Dunk Challenge" inspiring fans to dunk Oreos in milk to re-connect with their inner child. Let's not forget the heralded 100-day "Daily Twist" campaign to celebrate Oreo's 100 year anniversary in 2012. The heralded Oreo art inspired by cultural happenings included a rainbow Oreo supporting Gay Pride Month and a version to commemorate the Mars Rover landing -- with red filling and tire treads. And finally, hands-down, one of the most popular Super Bowl tweets ever reminding fans during the black-out of 2013 that "You can still dunk in the dark".

It is these emotive campaigns making you FEEL intrinsically connected to Oreo that generates impact, like a Facebook community of more than 42 million fans around the globe. In fact, Oreo ranks among the top 10 brand Facebook pages in the world! This emotional connection is exactly what sets a brand apart from a mere product. A brand has the power to transform a desire for a cookie into a craving for an Oreo. This craving then nags at their 42 million fans the next time they walk down the cookie aisle. It draws them like a magnet past all the "other cookies" until they are standing in front of the only cookie that can bring them the joy they seek. And there, right in the middle...the new, limited edition Birthday Cake Oreo's. Do they say, "$3.00 just for cookies? That's more than double those other cookies!" Not likely. Instead, these Oreo enthusiasts are relieved they found them. And then they stock up afraid the limited edition cookie could be sold out next time.

If you aren't a cookie fan, then maybe you are a water fan? With 60% of your body composed of it, who isn't? People who drink Smartwater will tell you it isn't just a product to quench your thirst. They will herald it as essential to support an active and demanding lifestyle... and then proceed to pay a 3-4x premium. People who swear by Post-It Notes (hand raised here) will tell you they help to organize and process their thoughts better than just generic paper (loose, spiral bound, yellow-legal pads, etc.). And with a clear conscience pay a 5-6x premium. Or, people who take their clothes to Tide Dry Cleaners. They will tell you Tide Dry Cleaners are experts in the care of garments unlike typical dry-cleaning services who just clean… and yep, pay a 2-4x premium.

Customers don't pay these premiums just once, they do so continually, feeding the virtuous cycle of love between the customer and brand forging a relationship hard to breach by competition. Think of it as a brand's version of "compounding interest". It's just like putting money into a savings account that earns interest. That dividend you yield gets reinvested back into the total, creating a bigger total generating more interest. With brands, the compounding is of customer advocacy. When customers become so passionately connected, they become evangelists with their beacons of love. This evangelism attracts more customers and their advocacy.

Yes, all of the examples are big, national brands…well, they are now, but, they didn't start that way. Every brand started from a place of anonymity, just a babe in the mind, sketch or prototype of its inventor. Then this babe grew and flourished in the hands of Brand-Love builders. These masters understood how to capitalize on the emotional connection people make with the brand at the right time and in the right way. If it were just about how much money thrown at it, don't you think all of the big hotel chains would have figured out how to contain Air BnB by now? Instead, Air BnB is the fastest growing hotel chain[4] and they don't even have brick-and-mortar hotels. They have accomplished this by selling a coveted experience versus just a place to sleep. Or, how about Dollar Shave Club's quest to get a share of what was thought to be an impenetrable razor blade market? The incumbents valued at several billion dollars each haven't been able to thwart their attack. Again,

Dollar Shave Club's emotionally motivated mission to connect with their customer prevails.

What all these businesses embrace that many under-value is that **since 90% of decision-making is based on emotion, what they must sell is a higher-order emotional benefit.** This enlightened mindset focuses on cultivating these connections with the hope they will evolve into full-fledged love. **Beloved brands attract more customers, drive more loyalty, and ultimately generate more impact. This creates** *tangible value* **which can command a higher price point and drive higher valuations. Therefore, it is critical for products to transform into brands.** If not, they will default to a commodity.

The commodity world is where purchase decisions are based on cold calculations of price/utility ratios. This puts you in an anonymous rat-race with your competition for survival. Remember "Interstate Cheap Price/Commodity" where the product with the lowest price (for the customer) and highest margins (for the retailer) wins? What's more, this position compromises your valuation for funding and exit strategies because there is no foundation for which to extrapolate future growth. Now, being a brand and having that solid emotional connection doesn't make you bullet-proof, but it is like going into a gun-fight with a Kevlar vest versus just taking your chances against the flying bullets. If you don't believe me, watch a few episodes of *Shark Tank* or *The Profit*. Study how they evaluate deals. Pay special attention to the rationale for Marcus Lemonis' decisions which transform the businesses he invests in. He is like the Dr. Ruth for companies.

So, how can you achieve this enlightened mindset espoused by these prolific Brand-Love builders? By redefining what is possible. Businesses existing within a commodity mindset believe their potential for generating revenue is limited. They lament, "My product isn't very sexy", "My customers only care about the price", "There is too much competition", etc. Businesses embracing a brand-building mindset believe there is unlimited potential for generating revenue. Instead of lamenting, they would question, "How do I make my product sexy?", "How do I get my customers to care about more than just the price?", "How do I drive more value than my competition?".

But, as Tom Bilyeu, co-founder of the billion-dollar brand, Quest Nutrition, says, "Having potential isn't the same as realizing it." The next chapter will focus on a proven framework for transforming from a product to a brand. It starts with helping you uncover unique brand insights relevant for your customer. This will allow you to authentically yet unexpectedly connect to your customer's heart and build those essential emotional connections. In doing so, you will create an ecosystem generating a virtuous cycle of Brand-Love, the spark essential to ignite your growth trajectory.

CHAPTER 3

HOW DO I KNOW WHEN I HAVE A BRAND?

You don't have a brand until you can explicitly and clearly articulate and validate:

1. Who am I?
2. Why am I different?
3. Why do you (the customer) want me?

This fundamental framework not only defines your brand identity (name, look, tag-line, equity choices, etc.) but also serves as a filter for strategic choices helping you cultivate Brand-Love to grow your business. This is why it is much better to do this work at the BEGINNING of your journey. But, if you have been traversing this path for awhile now, don't fret because we are going to make a course correction getting you on the "Super-Highway of Relevancy" and on your way to forging Brand-Love. But as I said before, you must be willing to embrace your inner Mark Zuckerberg and be prepared to break things.

I promised you a proven framework, so let's get to it. In order to address the big three: 1) Who am I? 2) Why am I different? 3) Why do you want me? you must first endure the quality thinking mentioned before. You may be surprised by the simplicity of the framework, but don't underestimate its power. It is hard to uncover high-potential customer insights allowing your brand to uniquely yet authentically connect to the heart, soul and mind. So, I am going to challenge you to dig deeper, be honest and hear the answers differently…and by differently I mean from the voice of your customers and what they require, not just what you have to offer them. I call this "What If…" Ideation. You can also think about it as the construction materials required to build your "Super-Highway of Relevancy" on which your Brand-Love vehicles will travel on. More on the vehicles later. For now, keep in mind that YOU are the construction worker in this analogy as well as the architect. So, put on your hard-hat, steel-toed boots and get ready to sweat. I am going to provide you the questions first and then address them in more detail. There is also space for you initial responses. We will reflect on these later so you can truly appreciate the transformation in mindset and actionable potential.

"What If…" Ideation

1. **Who is your target customer?** To be choiceful and intentional is critical. Questions to help you drive specificity here are outlined later.

_____

_____

_____

_____

_____

_____

Now, put yourself in your customer's shoes for the next questions (Note: Using "her" as a proxy, but this could be a "him" or "them" if your customer is a business). This may feel a bit awkward, but I do this intentionally to force you to think about it from her point-of-view which helps you confirm or deny your current assumptions. It also prevents defaulting into an advertising mentality tempting you to push your own agenda.

2. **What really causes me angst right now?** Identify real tensions and fears that can be turned around and become opportunities for your business to connect in authentic yet unexpected ways. This gives the product purpose.

_____

_____

_____

_____

_____

_____

_____

3. **What's the emotional impact the angst is having on me?** This is the emotion that comes with the tensions. Internalizing this will give you access to a higher-order benefit that drives Brand-Love.

_____

_____

_____

_____

_____

_____

_____

4. **What do I need from a product to address this?** Here you articulate "what-must-be-true" for your target customer to appreciate that your product is uniquely essential in solving the tension she's facing. Sometimes it is hard for customers to articulate this. So you will need to use your powers of observation, interpretation and reading-between-the-lines to ensure you have sufficiently addressed the skepticism.

_____

_____

_____

_____

_____

_____

5. **What signals/cues are essential to reinforce this is the right product for me?** Once you are clear on "what must be true" you define the robust support needed to drive believability.

_____

_____

_____

_____

_____

_____

Q1-5 answers
"Who am I?" and "Why am I different?"

6. **Who are the sources I trust? What do they need to say for me to believe it?** This helps you identify the first two components of the Brand-Love vehicle: the Story-Teller and the Message.

_____

_____

_____

_____

_____

_____

7. **Where and when am I going to be the most receptive?** This helps you identify the third and final component of your Brand-Love vehicle: the Engagement Point. This defines when and through what channel your customer will be the most receptive to what you defined in Q6.

_____

_____

_____

_____

_____

Q6-7 answers
"Why do you want me?"

8. **Does this transform my life for the better?** This evaluates your success in transforming the tension and negative emotion in Q2-3 into a Brand-Love connection ultimately resulting in positive and systemic business impact.

_____

_____

_____

_____

_____

Let's address each question in more detail:

1. Who is your target customer?

As mentioned above, it is critical to be choiceful and intentional in identifying your target customer. The biggest mistake businesses make here is to be too broad and too afraid of alienating or missing out on a customer. This is "Advertising" mentality, which does have a valid role in driving brand awareness. But it isn't really conducive to driving the emotional connections critical for cultivating Brand-Love. In trying to reach everybody, you really end up talking to nobody in effect turning you into a commodity. By now you should cringe whenever you read that word.

So, resist generic classifications of your target like "professionals with discretionary income" and instead do the due diligence to specify characteristics, passion points, interests, behaviors, life stages, etc. that create a tangible demographic to be engaged. In doing this, disruption is possible. Take for example the premium car industry. They all target professionals with discretionary income, so it is no surprise that the industry has coasted (pun intended) based on reputation alone. Then along comes Elon Musk who rocks the industry by positioning Tesla as an ultra-cool... tech company?!. He unapologetically targets cutting edge tech-junkies (aka. I need to have the latest toy NOW), who are also environmentally motivated movers-and-shakers. They enthusiastically jump into his vision of changing the world. When you purchase a Tesla, you are identifying yourself as one of his brethren and part of the ethos he has created. Instant status upgrade.

You may say Musk needs this level of targeting because he is selling a $70,000+ electricity-powered vehicle which is niche within an already niche market of "professionals with discretionary income". But there is no doubt he chooses to. He knows winning those early adopters will grow the popularity of the brand and in-turn pull in a substantial mainstream customer base resulting in a broader market; one that can now support the Model 3. Furthermore, Tesla has disrupted the auto industry in a way that hasn't been seen since Henry Ford introduced the Model T instead of attempting to breed faster horses.

Again, this isn't about the money invested or the cost of the product but making the intentional choice to target customers and relentlessly pursue them. I don't care if you are selling expensive cars, cupcakes, counter-tops or a squirrel-proof bird feeder (which has still yet to be invented), intentionally defining a target customer is key in developing a Brand-Love strategy that will uncap your business' potential.

If you need help in defining your target customer, approach it like you would an on-line dating profile. It makes sense that in order to build Brand-Love, you are going to need to date. I highly recommend for fast entry onto the "Super-Highway of Relevancy" you skip through the first few rounds where you embellish, generalize, and accept characteristics you are really not okay with and fast forward to the honest profile which will attract a good match. Otherwise, your business may come to the same tumultuous and abrupt end as those dates you pulled in by pretending to be something you're not. Below are prompts to get your brain working. Use as much detail as possible when describing:

1. Who uses the competition and why?

2. Who is most often making purchases of my product? Repeat purchases?

3. Who has purchased and never come back? Note: Sometimes knowing who is not your customer helps to refine who is.

4. Who lives/works in the area of your business? Note: This is helpful if you are a local shop where people come to you (i.e. restaurant, boutique, gym, salon, etc.)

5. Who has given you the most emotional reaction (good or bad) to your business?

After going through these prompts, you may find that you have several contenders as your target customer ranging from untapped segments of your existing customer base to an altogether brand new target. Choose one to start with...one that you believe has the highest potential to deliver your business goals. If you get through the entire process and determine you don't have sufficient reach, then choose a second target and go through the process again. Resist the urge to just expand your demographic unless your due diligence has revealed that there is enough over-lap (like 80%) that connects with both emotionally. The number of target customers you can manage at a time is really dependent on the capacity of your business, but it is best to sequentially roll out the action plans so not to over extend the business or under-develop the target.

2. What really causes me angst right now?

3. What's the emotional impact the angst is having on me?

Put yourself in the shoes of your customer and walk through a day in her life. If you can do this for real and not just as a cerebral exercise, even better. Allow yourself to feel what she feels as you go through the experience so you can identify real tensions that can become opportunities for your business. Tensions can be negative emotions or moments of discovery as in "Life would be so much better if I only had…". Resist the urge to jump to solutions at this point, as you are still in discovery mode.

To illustrate the point, let's consider how The Laundress, a boutique clothing care solution, may have internalized their customers' tension. Ironically, this story doesn't start in the laundry room, it starts standing in front of a women's closet and goes something like this… *"Where is that cashmere sweater that goes with this skirt?!"* she *shrieks in panic. "That sweater is the only one that goes with this skirt and I need it for my first date tonight. It is my go-to for guys I actually want to impress." As she is tearing apart her closet all of a sudden she remembers, "Nooooo! It is at the dry-cleaners!! They are closed. Now what am I going to wear?"* The angst she is feeling over not having THE sweater comes from an impassioned need for a specific outfit that helps her to feel a certain way. If it was just a functional need (i.e. I should wear a sweater because it is cold outside), the disappointment would abate quickly and she would simply make another unemotional choice. It is this higher-level emotional need thwarted by a care regimen over which she has no sense of control that created the opportunity for The Laundress.

In order to articulate the opportunity, you must first analyze the situation by asking "why". *Why* is she in this situation? *Why* is she feeling this way? Keep asking "Why?" until you get to a point where you can ask "What if…?". So going back to our fashionista longing for her sweater that completes her go-to outfit, the analysis looks like this:

- *Why* is she feeling this angst? Because she doesn't have a sweater that she really wants to wear.
- *Why* does she want that sweater? Because certain outfits make us feel good. When we feel good, we feel secure to take on important moments.
- *Why* doesn't she have the sweater? Because it is at the dry-cleaners.
- *Why* is it at the dry-cleaners? Because it is made of cashmere, and she doesn't feel comfortable washing it at home. She is afraid of ruining it as she spent more than she usually does on a sweater (i.e. investment piece).

Therefore:

- *What if* she had a product that does make her feel comfortable washing her cashmere sweater at home?

And here-in lies the opportunity which The Laundress refined into the following product statement: "<u>An eco-friendly, effective detergent able to wash delicate fabrics like wool, cashmere and silk</u> to reduce dry cleaning." A purpose is born.

To ensure your purpose is sufficient, cover up your product name and insert the name of your competition. If it is still plausible, you haven't dug deep enough to uncover a meaningfully differentiated purpose. For example, The Laundress clearly identifies who they are in the product statement (single underlined above); however, this same product statement wouldn't be surprising to hear coming from their competitors. If this was only it, you may conclude that The Laundress is just one small part of the commoditized world of laundry detergents. But it is the addition of the claim to "reduce dry cleaning" (double underlined above) that feels novel. It triggers emotional salvation - my clothes will be in my closet, ready when I want them.

Now be aware that when you start offering novelty, you also invite skepticism. This is normal and why the process has five more questions to address.

4. What do I need from a product to address this?

5. What signals/cues/context do I need to reinforce this is the right product for me?

These questions address the skepticism introduced by the novelty. In Q4, you are seeking "what must be true" so your target customer will choose your product, and ONLY your product, as the solution to the tension she is facing. In Q5, you are defining the support needed to drive believability. This logic then becomes a narrative from which all of your communications are derived. Its message captures your customer's attention and hooks them in by compellingly articulating "Who am I?" and "Why am I different?".

Let's go back to my example of The Laundress and see how the Founders may have contemplated Q4. If they asked themselves "what must be true" for my customer to believe that The Laundress is "An eco-friendly, effective detergent able to wash delicate fabrics like wool, cashmere and silk to reduce dry-cleaning," they had to come to this conclusion:

- Our product must be made from ingredients that were (or perceived to be) gentle and non-toxic. Dry cleaners are expected to take great care with delicate items even though, ironically, they use chemical agents to clean the garments.

- Our product must leave the garment looking, smelling and feeling clean wash-after-wash without damage. That, after all, is the job of a good detergent.

- Our product must feel premium because dry-cleaned garments are frequently more expensive investment pieces. If the product looks cheap, nobody will believe it can care appropriately for the garment.

- There must be some element of expertise to credential our product. Otherwise, why would anyone trust our product over the dry-cleaners?

With the "what must be true" statements established, let's move into Q5 and unpack the choices The Laundress made to build believability for each:

<u>The product must be made with ingredients
perceived to be gentle and non-toxic.</u>

"Eco-friendly" signals gentle, but The Laundress corroborates its claim with transparency. They list their ingredients with each product descriptor on their order page of their website. Plus, they add reassurances that the detergent is "nontoxic, biodegradable, and allergen-free" as well as "free of petroleum, phosphate, phthalates, and artificial color". They further add that the products are "Cruelty-free with no animal by-products" and just to make sure you know they walk the talk, "All The Laundress products are tested on Gwen & Lindsey (The Founders)". These claims are all reinforced visually with a very simple and clean package with translucent, soft colors. Gentle...check.

<u>It must leave the garment looking, smelling and feeling clean,
wash-after-wash without damage to the garment.</u>

To reinforce the detergent's effectiveness, The Laundress has created customized products for specialty garments like "Wool &

Cashmere Shampoo" giving confidence that the product was formulated especially for those textiles. This is supported by an extensive and sophisticated "How To..." search engine on their website providing explanations for every textile. Also, they recommend stain removal methods just in case. This is also how they establish expertise. The only additional support they could have provided is a side-by-side comparison of garments dry-cleaned versus cared for at home with The Laundress. Arguably, this is almost redundant based on the rigor of the other components. Effective...check.

<u>It must feel premium because these dry-cleaned garments are frequently more expensive investment pieces.</u>

This impression requires a well conceptualized and consistently executed style guide. A style guide is an asset accounting of design attributes that visually represent the desired look, tone, and feel of your product and eventually your brand. This is key in ensuring your customers can easily identify and attribute the product they want to only you and your purpose. Peruse The Laundress' website, engage in their social handles or visit their store, to see consistency across all touch-points. The visual presentation of the products including the way they are represented in imagery and the situational context is all carefully curated to feel upscale, premium and luxurious. Not at all like buying a bottle of laundry detergent at the grocery store with a coupon. Premium...check.

<u>There needs to be some element of expertise to credential the product.</u>

Beyond the expertise reinforcing the effectiveness of the product, two other pillars of expertise make the product credible. The first is the Founders story: Gwen Whiting and Lindsey Boyd came from luxury fashion companies. Working in fashion leads one to believe they are skilled in the care of it as well. They underwrite this with frequent social media appearances in fashionable yet approachable contexts.

The second pillar of expertise is life. The Laundress has extended product offerings and content in ancillary spaces like Home Organization. By offering additional utility, not only do they create incremental ways-in to their products, they grow their credibility as someone who understands me – who is very much like me. Experts…check.

All of the proof-points and credibility builders are interwoven into a narrative. As with their style attributes, you will find this narrative pulled through all communication touch-points. Look at this excerpt from an article in *Fashionista*[5] covering the launch of their first flagship store in SoHo in December of 2015:

> *It's the first U.S. flagship for The Laundress, the only brand of cleaning products that I think can reasonably be described as luxurious. The store certainly feels more like a high-end boutique than, say, a Duane Reade.*
>
> *Longtime friends Gwen Whiting and Lindsey Boyd founded The Laundress 14 years ago after both feeling a bit stuck in their respective jobs at luxury fashion companies. Having already conceptualized the products — eco-friendly, effective detergents able to wash delicate fabrics like wool, cashmere and silk to reduce dry cleaning.*

Or, how about these excerpts from *Fast Company*[6] in January 2019:

> *Back in 2004, the concept behind a little startup called The Laundress seemed kind of crazy: The brand pitched itself as a luxurious, fashionable laundry detergent company in a world where most people bought inexpensive grocery store brands. But 15 years later, The Laundress is a global phenomenon, creating a lifestyle brand around humble home cleaning products. The*

Laundress's 51,000 followers on Instagram avidly scan pictures of marble-floored laundry rooms stocked with the brand's white bottles of detergent, and racks of sparkly party outfits about to be laundered. ...Before they started the company,

The Laundress's founders were hustling in their jobs in the luxury fashion industry, with Whiting serving as a senior designer at Ralph Lauren and Boyd as a manager for Chanel's Ready-to-Wear division. They noticed an odd gap in the market. While consumers were willing to invest a lot of money in beautifully tailored jeans and designer T-shirts, they would go home and launder these outfits using the same old run-of-the-mill detergents–Tide, All, Gain–that they had purchased from Target or Walgreens. Alternatively, they would send their clothes to dry cleaners where the garments would be exposed to toxic chemicals, and would often come back in worse shape than before.

"Our fundamental premise was that you don't need to send your clothes to the dry cleaners," says Whiting. "We focused on creating different formulas for different types of fabric, which was different from many detergents that have a one-size-fits-all approach."

They had the unorthodox idea to create a brand that had all the marks of a luxury brand: higher-quality ingredients, a focus on elegant design, and a superior customer experience. And yes, the price would also be higher.

Even in just these two articles, the narrative representing the "what-must-be-true" needs is consistently reinforced. But this doesn't happen by accident. You need to create vehicles to transport these themes to your target customer when and where she is receptive. This brings us to Q6 and Q7.

6. Who are the sources I trust? What do they need to say for me to believe it?

7. Where and when am I going to be the most receptive?

If Q2-5 is the infrastructure of your "Super-Highway of Relevancy", Q6 and 7 identify the "Brand-Love vehicles" and the route that will transport your narrative comprising the "what-must-be-true" proof-points to the heart, mind and soul of your customer. They answer "Why do you want me?". Many brand marketers are tempted to jump right to this step as they feel the most comfortable with "tactics", but then they are overwhelmed by the

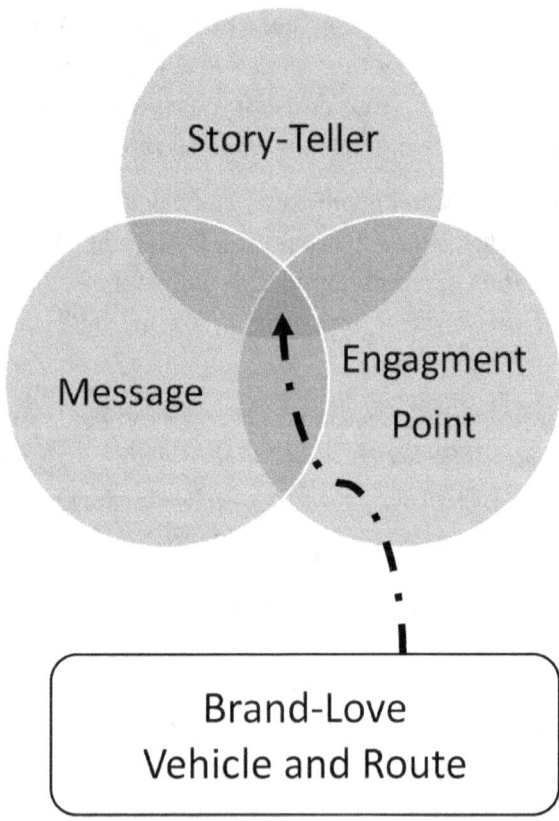

wide-range of choices as to what they could do and what they could say. Because you diligently worked through Q1-5, you have a robust filter to make those decisions. Now, don't get confused. This doesn't mean you have a brand yet. I call them "Brand-Love vehicles" to trigger the mindset shift required of you to transform your product into a brand.

Brand-Love vehicles and their route are derived at the intersection of three components:

1. **The Story-Teller:** This is the trusted source who delivers the message. In the "Brand-Love vehicle" analogy, this is the driver.

2. **The Message:** This is the Story-Teller's version of your narrative. It must effectively convey your "what must be true" proof-points but in the voice of your Story-Teller to maintain authenticity. These are like the features of your Brand-Love vehicle.

3. **The Engagement Point:** When and through what channel my customer will be the most receptive to a love connection. This is choosing the fastest lane and most ideal conditions for the Brand-Love vehicle to travel.

For you visual learners, it looks like this:
Let's take a deeper diver into each one.

The Story-Teller

There are 3 primary types of Story-Tellers:

- <u>The Product</u> — This often takes the form of advertising (e.g. TV, digital, radio, press releases, etc.) or outreach on product-owned channels like a website or social channels.

- An Influencer — Many people associate "influencers" with just bloggers or social media mavens. But I encourage a broader definition to include: celebrities, athletes, professional experts, media personalities, and even politicians. But the largest yet most nebulous influencing source is the one closest to the customer...their friends and family.

- A 3rd-Party Property — These can be pop-culture inspired (e.g. NFL, Academy of Country Music), Professional or Special Interest Organizations (e.g. American Academy of Dermatology, World Wildlife Fund), Philanthropies, and even Retailers. Often-times, these partnerships take the form of sponsorships/endorsements or buy-ins. The other opportunity is credentials which come in the form of awards and seals from trusted sources like: The Good Housekeeping Seal, Allure Best of Beauty, and JD Power.

In order to select a Story-Teller, you must first clarify who is the most credible source for your message. Which leads to the next component of the Brand-Love vehicle.

Messaging

Customers perceive and react to Story-Tellers differently. So, it is vital to question who would be the most effective Story-Teller to drive believability of your message. The below outlines typical Messaging for each Story-Teller:

- The Product – Best for delivering foundational product information, i.e., purpose, new product releases, performance claims/demos and promotions such as special deals or incentives. Often times this type of messaging is referred to as "push" messaging because of its one way direction -- from the product to the customer. The benefit: the product message can be hyper-focused. But if over-used, your customer may feel like they are in a relationship with someone who only likes to talk about themselves.

- An Influencer – Best for delivering more editorial style messaging. Influencers provide a real-life context and experience that makes the product more relatable. Often this results in compelling endorsements and testimonials. The benefit is influencers can reach and engage your target customer more authentically than you can. However, because you are borrowing the equity and good-faith of the influencer to enhance your own credibility, your messaging will need to be finessed to authentically come from the voice of the influencer. Don't make the mistake of expecting your influencer to recite your product messaging.

- A 3rd-Party Property– Best to deliver credibility behind your messaging. Like influencers, the benefit is you're building trust through association. In addition, they generally have highly recognizable and compelling assets (e.g. logos/ marks, talent - spokespeople or spokesanimals, awards, seals, events, etc.) that when paired smartly with your Product and Influencer messaging show-up as endorsements. This can accelerate believability. These properties also tend to have large followings on their own platforms which you can tap to reach your target customer at scale. The watch-out here is the property is almost always the top-biller making your messaging secondary. If there isn't an intrinsic link, your product could get lost.

If you are still confused as to whom your Story-Teller should be, ask yourself the following:

- If I were in my customer's shoes, which Story-Teller would I be more apt to believe?
- Which Story-Teller would be the most convincing to get me to buy the product?

Then pick one. This is an art not a science. So, don't expect a master formula to show you the way. You are going to have to learn how to live with a bit of ambiguity.

Engagement Point

This is the final piece of the Brand-Love puzzle. It guides your choices so your Brand-Love vehicle has the clearest, most direct path possible to your target customer. Mission critical, your message must penetrate her daily deluge of information overload. Trying to reach her where and when she isn't receptive is like trying to drive your Brand-Love vehicle through torrential rainfall. Strive for the most ideal conditions possible: clear skies and open lanes. This typically means being where she is already. Here are typical Engagement Points for each Story-Teller:

- The Product – As mentioned above, advertising is the most typical route with TV still the dominate channel. Digital is on the rise but is notoriously difficult to navigate due to the ever-changing landscape and algorithms. The new entertainment formats like OTT (over-the-top) programming (i.e. Netflix, Hulu, Streaming, etc.) are a new frontier but largely still remain an ad-free zone. Some products are flirting with product placement integrations inside popular shows and movies. Product messages also dominate at point-of-sale (POS). This includes retailer brick-and-mortar as well as on-line presences and even direct-to-consumer (DTC). You may even have your own flagship store. Finally, it is typical for a business to develop its social media channels to serve as Engagement Points. A calendar which plans content and timing is highly recommended.

- An Influencer – Influencer messages are best received on the influencer's channels. These include, social media, blogs, editorial articles, forums, appearances, interviews, speeches, white-papers, workshops, etc. In the case of friends and family, much of the messaging gets communicated less formally via small group gatherings or even 1:1. The hope here is to create a word-of-mouth ground-swell. Don't be surprised if you have to pitch (especially editorial) or contract and pay for influencers. It could be well worth the cost because influencers normally invite two-way communication which builds relationships.

- A 3ʳᵈ-Party Property – As mentioned, these partnerships generally take the form of sponsorships or buy-ins. Popular sponsorship opportunities include: sporting events, festivals, concerts, conferences, parties/celebrations, etc. Certain retailers can also serve in this capacity as you will see in the examples below. Opportunity also lies in what surrounds the events like social media chatter, promotional materials, newsletters and publications. The two most common places for credentialed messaging is: 1) Where your influencer and product messaging appears, and 2) On the organizations platform. For the former, this could be posting on your social media handles that you will be at a special event launching your new product. For the latter, it is the event posting on their social media that everyone should stop by and try your new product. Awards and seals are generally earned either through pro-active application or via an internal process governed by the organization. They too can be leveraged in the two places outlined above.

Now that you understand the type of components that make up Brand-Love vehicles, the challenge becomes choosing the right ones to deliver your proof-points. To effect this, let's look at a few examples from The Laundress. Keep in mind too that you may be able to use the same Brand-Love vehicle to deliver multiple proof-points.

Let's consider how The Laundress might have built a Brand-Love vehicle based on these proof-points: 1) The product needs to be made with ingredients perceived to be gentle and non-toxic; and 2) It needs to leave the garment looking, smelling and feeling clean and undamaged wash-after-wash. Though their website offers in-depth information on both these topics as previously discussed, the question now becomes: "Is the Product the most believable Story-Teller"? After all, they were new and yet to establish their own credibility. Who was going to take them at their word? And, with an under-developed social following, there just wasn't enough fans to receive the message.

Instead, The Laundress turned to a rather unexpected Influencer Story-Teller: music super-star, John Mayer. John was a self-proclaimed fan of the product, even posting his own "how-to" videos on caring for his clothes using the products. This testimonial was exactly what The Laundress needed to authentically translate their proof-points into Messaging their target customer would be receptive to. And because John posted these tutorials on his own channels, the Message was received by his multitude of loyal fans. To fully maximize the effectiveness of this Influencer Engagement Point, The Laundress amplified by posting simultaneously on their Product social media channels pulling the fans sideways into their own Engagement Points. What's more, The Laundress collaborated with John to create a signature scent becoming a highly effective call-to-action to visit yet another Product Engagement Point, The Laundress' website and boutique store. Brand-Love vehicle created!

But why was this so effective? The truth comes in asking the question "Why do you want me?"

Many would answer this question with "Because John Mayer uses it." I would agree there are folks where that is enough. But celebrity fandom is rarely sufficient to grow massive appeal. It may be good for a blip in purchase, but it is fleeting. What truly made this Brand-Love vehicle effective was John's personal passion for the product which translated into a compelling testimonial at scale. This intrigued multitudes of people beyond John Mayer fans. This is called being "popular". "Because I am popular" is of significantly more value than John's celebrity status when answering the question "Why do you want me?". This is because the "popularity" Brand-Love vehicle can be revived with other Story-Tellers, Messages and Engagement Points as the customer landscape evolves or the proof-points change. A Brand-Love vehicle created solely on someone's celebrity status has a short life even as "celebrity" can have a short life. You don't want your product to die with it.

Let's look at another example just to make sure you can internalize this because Q6-7 requires advanced brand-building thought. What about: 1) An element of expertise to credential the product; and 2) It needs to feel premium because dry-cleaned garments are frequently more expensive investment pieces.

The need for a credential triggers the pursuit of a 3rd-Party Property Story-Teller. In this case, The Laundress turned to the first place their customer would likely be contemplating the care of a garment: a Retailer. But not just any Retailer. Because of the need to feel premium, the Laundress forged a partnership with Bloomingdales, seller of high-end, dry-cleaned garments and by default experts in their care. There, the Message and Engagement Point was a recommendation to add The Laundress to your order at point-of-sale (POS). Just this simple suggestion from an expert at a time the customer is most receptive can drive instantaneous trust and connection. Brand-Love vehicle created!

But like John Mayer, this Brand-Love vehicle doesn't solely rely on Bloomingdales to go. Wouldn't Nordstrom's or Neiman Marcus also be compelling? So, in asking the question "Why does she want me?", it isn't just because Bloomingdales trusts it. It is because "Premium Retailers" trust it. Again, this elevates your thinking from a mere isolated tactic to an approach that can drive scale.

Now, don't make false assumptions that a "popularity" or "trusted by premium retailers" Brand-Love vehicle must operate like a flashy red Ferrari that revs 0-60 mph in 3 seconds. This vehicle will burn through cash like the sports-car burns through fuel... quickly. It will also be expensive to maintain. You may be surprised to hear that these Brand-Love vehicles can be effective even as luxury or even more practical sedans as well. How do you decide?

By articulating what success look like through Key Performance Indicators (KPI's) in consideration of your budget. These metrics help you set expectations for what is possible with the dollars available. And once activated, will give you feedback on whether your Brand-Love vehicle is effectively moving you towards your business goals or needs refining.

The more quantitative the metrics, the easier it is to objectively measure success. And success can only be determined if you have clear benchmarks to measure against. These benchmarks could be yours (e.g. increase in sales, increase in customers or social following). Or, the benchmarks could be derived externally from the industry (e.g. social platform standards, percent of a target demographic), third party agencies (e.g. ranking or awards), the category you are in (e.g. market share data) or maybe even an aspirational category (e.g. Tom Bilyeu benchmarks against Disney for his production studio). Also critical is to set a time frame in which you expect to achieve the success as this will also factor into the make and model of your Brand-Love vehicle.

So, what KPI's might The Laundress have established for its "popularity" Brand-Love vehicle being driven by John Mayer? Knowing that popularity is the marriage of reach and positive sentiment, key KPI's could have looked like:

KPI	What a Successful Brand-Love vehicle Looks Like
Total amount of people reached through all Engagement Points	**Grows exposure (reach).** To make this more actionable, The Laundress may benchmark this versus their current exposure (i.e. double, triple, etc.) or versus industry (i.e. % of women) in their target customer demographic. So: **Double exposure within current demographic target.** Or, **Reach 25% of Bloomingdale's female shoppers.**
Social community health	**Thriving social community (indicative of positive sentiment).** Like in the above, The Laundress may benchmark versus their current fan following and engagements (i.e. triple the number of followers, double likes, shares, positive comments, etc.) or possibly against an aspirational target (i.e. Brand X's fan following and engagement rates). So: **Double fan following and shares on Instagram.** Or, **Consistently achieve Facebook likes equivalent to Brand X's best post.**
Sales	There could be several ways of analyzing success here: **Sku productivity** (i.e. Delivers incremental sales while minimizing cannibalization) **Positive Return-on-Investment** (ROI) **Positive Sales Halo** (i.e. The new sku drives an increase in purchase of other products in the portfolio as well).

Certainly, these KPI's would tempt most to choose a Ferrari. But understanding that driving systemic popularity (and not just the blips mentioned earlier) doesn't happen over-night, The Laundress made a different choice. Because it is essential for the vehicle to make good time, be highly efficient so the budget will stretch, and still be cool enough for John Mayer, The Laundress opted more for a Lexus Hybrid.

How does this show-up differently? For example, instead of going for a high-cost, glitzy launch event at an expensive NYC establishment (Ferrari), they choose a posh, in-store event at their boutique (Lexus Hybrid). The first may take all your cash for one moment-in-time. The second can leave you enough cash for future moments, giving you more time to leverage your investment and deliver upon your KPI's.

In contrast, the KPI's for the "trusted by premium retailers" Brand-Love vehicle may look quite different. Here, the key KPI would be relationship based. Maybe something like: "Maintain value driven partnerships resulting in high-profile exposure at POS." Though preserving relationships requires on-going attention, once established, processes help to make the effort more predictable and planned. This Brand-Love vehicle looks more like a Honda Accord – cost-effective and runs forever with regularly scheduled maintenance.

As your "Super-Highway of Relevancy" starts filling up with your fleet of Brand-Love vehicles, you need to carefully plan their itineraries. You can then control the traffic on the channels and keep the vehicles from stalling and jamming up your highway. Q7 "Where and when am I going to be the most receptive?" helps you make choices so that all of your Brand-Love vehicles have the clearest, most direct path possible to your target consumer. **In order to effectively manage traffic, you must start thinking about your "Super-Highway of Relevancy" as an ecosystem that surrounds your target consumer.** Here, your Brand-Love vehicles work like a community, moving cooperatively with each other but also with her world to engage her more comprehensively thus creating moments of relevancy. In these moments, she chooses you. **When your ecosystem is productive, the love for you product grows, striding you closer to brand status.** Recall, beloved brands attract more customers, drive more loyalty, and ultimately generate more impact. This creates *tangible value* which can command a higher price point and drive higher valuations. Remember Oreo?

Let's consider one of the most productive brand ecosystems ever created...Apple. An iPhone user will give up coffee forever rather than switch phones. Why? If they gave up their iPhone, they would need to learn a new operating system [groan], which doesn't sync with their MacBook [longer groan]. Worse, they panic of being unable to access all of their photos stored on the cloud, their downloaded iTunes, the info on their apps, or even a reason to go to the Apple store. Then the clincher....can I no longer get my texts on my wrist?! [Mental break-down] They plead: "Please don't take my iPhone! I am in way too deep. Take anything else." If you think I am being dramatic, ask an iPhone user what it would take to get them to switch... and watch the anxiety set-in. Then try it again with a non-iPhone user and watch the difference. This is the power of an ecosystem. Apple masterfully orchestrates their Brand-Love vehicles to deliver their proof-points when and where their customers are receptive...and equally as masterful at getting them to work cooperatively so their customers cannot live without them. They have become life sustaining.

For example, Apple's retail locations serve two primary Brand-Love vehicles: "Technology Innovators" and "Customer Service". These stores radiate the vibe of silicone valley reincarnated with their sleek look, presentation of tempting gadgets galore, and tech experts who make you feel so welcome. Though you may hear about the release of Apple's new iPhone technology through other channels, it is at the store where you can interface with it directly. This environment awakens the kid in all of us who now wants the toy she is playing with so joyfully. But what makes the new toy something you need now versus something you put on your wish list for later? Well, it just so happens you are at the Apple store hoping one of the expert technicians will explain why your iPhone has been acting funny. It turns out, your phone can't support the latest iOS system upgrade which is limiting its functionality frustrating you to no end. But hope is not lost! As your technician, now brilliantly disguised as a sales person, reveals that the latest iPhone can fix your problems. That is all you need to be convinced. The ecosystem prevails!

Spend time mapping out your ecosystem. Consider the effectiveness of each Brand-Love vehicle through the lens of the KPI's and its impact on others. Look for potential collisions and traffic jams as well as synergies that can work like car-pool lanes. The final question will help you determine if your fleet of Brand-Love vehicles are collectively generating a productive ecosystem essential for substantial business growth.

8. Does this transform my life for the better?

This question addresses the impact of your fleet of Brand-Love vehicles and whether the ecosystem has been successful in addressing Q2 and Q3: "What really causes me angst right now?" and "What's the emotional impact the angst is having on me?". In other words, have you effectively translated your "What-Must-Be-True" narrative to make a love connection? For The Laundress, it comes down to whether they successfully instilled the confidence their target customer needs to care for her expensive investment pieces at home. And if the pleasure of now having these cherished garments in her closet when she wants them is enough of a love connection to purchase and re-purchase The Laundress. Affirmative responses confirm the Brand-Love vehicles created a productive ecosystem allowing them to reach their destination and hard-wire into their customers' heart, mind and soul.

Just as with each of your Brand-Love vehicles, KPI's are also assigned to objectively evaluate the effectiveness of the Brand-Love vehicle collective, or ecosystem. Since there are no direct measurements for "hard-wired love connections", The Laundress likely tracked <u>signals</u> of a successful love connection. For example:

- <u>Overall sales and volume growth.</u> Is she rewarding The Laundress with her purchase? Over-time, is she repeating her purchase and increasing the number of products she is purchasing? Are price-points being maintained or even increasing?
- <u>Market-share growth.</u> Is she choosing The Laundress INSTEAD of the competition?
- <u>Global expansion.</u> Is her evangelism creating interest from customers in other countries creating new markets?
- <u>Portfolio expansion.</u> Is she clamoring for new product offerings both within and outside the fabric care category?
- <u>Increased credibility.</u> Are reputable Story-Tellers organically advocating for the brand and seeking out The Laundress desiring their partnership and expertise?

In demonstrating sustained success in the above (not just a fluke win), the ultimate goal of The Laundress or any start-up can be realized: an ecosystem where Brand-Love compounds, creating enough tangible value to transform a product into a brand. The big three: 1) Who am I? 2) Why am I different? 3) Why do you want me? are articulated and validated. And with that, doors that were once closed begin to open. On the other side are deep-pocket investors, big-box retailers for wholesaling, expansion opportunities, and for some, the ultimate…a BigCo buy-out.

For 15 years, The Laundress created Brand-Love vehicles to travel down the "Super-Highway of Relevancy" with some reaching their destination and successfully connecting with the hearts, minds and souls of their target customers and some not. The Founders claim it took five years of steady sales and volume growth before the business reached an inflection point where they doubled revenue annually.[7] It is likely that this inflection point also marked surpassing another important threshold...validating their ecosystem and transforming from a product to a brand. Yet still, it was another 10 years of activating the brand's ecosystem to effect the level of global and portfolio expansion as well as the credibility shift needed to trigger the ultimate prize...a reported $100 million buyout of their brand by Unilever in January 2019.[8]

As you reflect on The Laundress' journey, some of you are going to balk at the amount of effort and time it took for the payout. You are going to think: "Certainly there must be an easier and quicker way?". Here is where I remind you of the important realities I stated in the beginning:

- Your "Super-Highway of Relevancy" may not be the shortest route but it could be the most direct and sustainable route to realize your business' potential.
- It is going to be hard. That is why most businesses don't do it and inevitability don't realize their potential.
- Brands that intentionally choose to cultivate Brand-Love tend to be the ones that persevere and prosper.

Now it is your turn. Put these eight questions into practice for your own business so that you can clearly articulate "Who am I?", "Why am I different?" and "Why do you want me?" Compare the work you do here to your original responses when the questions were first presented. Recognize and embrace how your thinking has shifted to a new realm of business potential. Feel the swagger of having an infrastructure that will help you develop an action plan to realize that potential. Orchestrate your ecosystem and watch as Brand-Love compounds, creating tangible mass such that your product transforms into a brand. Enjoy how your beloved brand attracts more customers, drives more loyalty, and generates more impact. Seize the opportunity when the doors open for you.

CHAPTER 4

HOW TO BUILD BRAND-LOVE ON A START-UP BUDGET

How many times as you were going through the process did you censor yourself because "you didn't have money for that?" Keep in mind, The Laundress started their business in their "garage" like many of you have done. They poured their own money into their concept like I am sure you have done. And, they never took on VC funding…whaaaat?! I say all of this to make the point that building Brand-Love can be forged on any budget. But you must be smart about it. Here are some tips on how to do just that:

- Put it in the Budget: Build in your "Super-Highway of Relevancy" from the beginning. You will never be able to afford it if it isn't in your P&L. Some like to call this line item *marketing*. That's fine as long as you consider the budget for the building and execution. Just including executables like media or ad spends isn't sufficient. Without the strategy, you will have no guidelines of what and how to spend it. If you are struggling to tab how much, a good rule is 10% of your total revenue.

- Opportunistic Affinity: Look for brand ambassadors who already like you. Have your Google alerts on and spend time

1-2 times a week searching your brand and brand channels (i.e. your hashtags, feeds, etc.) to see who is talking about you. You may be surprised (as The Laundress was with John Mayer) to find that you have passionate fans with clout who would be thrilled to work with you. And because they are already advocates, they could be more amenable to value exchange deals, i.e. the exchange of assets versus money. These Band-Lovers become stronger, more authentic endorsers resulting in a better ROI. They even may be willing to alter their fee structure.

- Pilot and then Scale: Enter the pool from the shallow end and first learn how to tread water. Many are tempted to jump into the deep end with ankle weights where they struggle until they tire. We have all been there, and we all know what happens then. It is fine to cast a wide net to see what could work, but do so in a fiscally responsible way. Then, when results show what is working, double down on those successes and cut the rest. For example, the "What if..." process has revealed that a few influencers are necessary to drive your Brand-Love vehicles. Instead of jumping into multiple influencer contracts, you may choose to buy one or two posts from an influencer that fits your profile. Activate these first and see how they perform against your KPI's. Now you can test-and-learn on a lower risk investment. Yes, you may pay a premium for these posts, but I guarantee it is cheaper than multiple influencer contracts that you can't get out of down the road. The catch here is that your pilot needs to be scalable. A big mistake some brands make (even big name brands) is undermining the process by creating an artificial environment that doesn't truly mimic the larger opportunity for the sake of saving money. If the approach can't appropriately be piloted, find an alternate way to screen its potential before investing.

- <u>Network: Freelancers are your friends.</u> Entrepreneurship has not just sparked those with product ideas and a dream. The spark has also motivated those who have spent a first career in a corporate office learning their trade and now want to take their own talents and abilities beyond those doors (ahem). The benefit to you is BigCo and agency experience at a price you can afford. Become prolific on LinkedIn where these freelancers tend to engage, and do your homework to ensure they have the capabilities and experience you need. Ask for case studies either written or verbal, portfolios of work, start-up experience, etc. You should be able to find an expert to fulfill every need while you are in the start-up phase.

  Your network of expert freelancers also help deliver cost-savings so that the hiring of full-time personnel can be postponed. Generally, you don't need full-timers in many of the specialized areas of expertise during the start-up phase. And for some roles...never. So, why should you assume the over-head if you don't have to? Especially when you can afford to freelance top talent but probably not hire them? Hold out until you reach a brand threshold that demands this expansion. Hopefully you can then afford the expertise your brand requires.

- <u>Do your due diligence: Ensure agencies have experience working with start-ups.</u> This could be your first big expense outside of product development, manufacturing and distribution. I have seen too many start-ups exploited by big agencies who don't have the infrastructure or the desire to scale appropriately for them. So when it is time to contract an agency, it is important to do your due diligence by ensuring they:

- Can provide case studies of similar clients in your stage of development and budget constraints that have yielded a successful outcome. This gives you some confidence that the agency has the right mindset to approach your business challenges.

- Have an established infrastructure to support start-ups. This is especially important if you are attracted to agencies who serve BigCo's. These agencies are extensively staffed to support big programs with large budgets – out of a start-ups price range. You can't afford this, and what's more, these may not be the experts you need. Also, don't assume the opposite to be true either, i.e. a smaller agency is somehow a kindred spirit. Many times these agencies are founded on a core competency (e.g. social media) but will try to extend revenue by offering additional scope even if it isn't in their wheel-house. To avoid either trap, it is imperative you personally vet who will be on your team at the very beginning. You want resources who can be scrappy yet effective, as well as have deep expertise and talents into areas important to your growth. Additionally, they must be comfortable working in a dynamic environment and are doers not just thinkers. Their structure should enable direct engagement with each team member. Even if the agency chooses to assign a client-lead to manage the work, they should not be the "gate-keepers". Insist on meeting with your team regularly, and be bold in asking for different resources if your requirements are not met.

- Demand they commit to full cooperation, i.e. to work within your scope, budget and timing specifications. Your budget may not afford 100% assignment of resources on your business, but what you can command is delivery of what is promised, on budget and on time. These should be clearly defined in a brief and signed off on in a "Scope-of-Work" (SOW – also called a "Proposal" or "Statement-of-Work" or "Contract"). This leads to the next point…

- The Statement-of-Work (SOW) will only be as good as your brief. Be fully prepared to take the time to appropriately brief your contractors -- freelancers or agencies -- with the necessary details including but not limited to:

  - Background/Overview: A short statement providing the rationale for the SOW as well as any pertinent information which will inform the work.

  - Details about your Target Customer: Bring to life your target customer so everyone understands her as well as you do.

  - Deliverables and Timing: Outlines what is to be delivered by the contractor (i.e. strategy, action plan, execution activity, etc.) and on what timing.

  - Success Metrics: Clearly defined KPI's and impact measures. The more quantitatively specific the better.

  - Mandatories: As it implies, these are must-haves for the work.

  - Budget: Sets parameters for the size and extent of the work. This should include fees as well as out-of-pocket (OOP – sometimes called "pass-through") costs.

  - Signatures: Critical in ensuring all necessary parties are aligned to the terms of the brief.

The contractor then translates the brief into a SOW which becomes the official contract (also called a "Service Agreement"). This is signed by both of you as indisputable and mutually agreeable. The clearer your brief is the tighter the SOW will be, leaving little room for re-interpretation down the road. The unfortunate hazards of a vague brief: your contractor spending your capital -- money and precious time -- on activity you don't want.

For example, be wary of indefinite terms like "Brainstorms", "Landscape Assessments" or requests for significant on-boarding time. These activities are generally viewed as incremental budget line-items. In addition, because they often are part of the contractor's internal processes, they are hard to control and monitor by you. So, make sure they are time, budget and deliverable bound within an existing line-item or as a separate line-item, like: *$500 for a 1 week vetting of 3-5 prospective launch cities that meets the following criteria..."*

In fact, within the contract and subsequent billing, make sure ALL payment terms are affixed to key deliverables or success metrics. This keeps your contractors solely focused on what is most important for your business as well as what you are going to pay. A level of expectation is firmly established as to what a positive outcome looks like and holds them accountable for THAT outcome. When I hear the woes of start-ups who invested a lot of money in contractors to end-up with nothing in return, it is often due to a lack of prerequisite due diligence in selecting the right contractors (previous bullet). Or, it is because of a loosely defined brief that morphed into a nebulous contract with payment terms that didn't set the start-up with any leverage when results didn't meet expectations. The old bromide works here -- when you "assume"...you lose money. Well...that isn't exactly how it goes, but it is what will happen.

- <u>Get creative in the compensation</u>. If your cash flow is limited and your margins permit it, consider trying to negotiate a royalty or commission versus a straight fee for service. Freelancers especially could be amenable to such terms as it provides a nice upside when you are successful together. And per the above, it incentivizes contractors to sell your product. Retainers, or paying a contractor in installments (usually monthly) could also be a good option. Consider this if your scope needs flexibility for revision and optimization as you learn from pilots. Just be sure you are clear on what is included and not included in the retainer and that retainer meets YOUR needs first.

Hopefully you are feeling more confident that you can now afford to build Band-Love no matter your financial circumstances. So, now let's address how to ensure you have the right people with the right mindset on your construction team to build your "Super-Highway of Relevancy".

♥

CHAPTER 5

ESTABLISHING A
BRAND-LOVE TEAM

You will first want to identify a Core Team who will be the creators, operators and purveyors of your Brand-Love strategy. Members of your Core Team include a:

- <u>Director or Leader</u>: Manages the people on the team as well as the activities ensuring all work is harmonious, fluid and appropriately resourced to come in on budget and on deadline.
- <u>Strategist</u>: Designs and manages the Brand-Love process and has the right mindset to lead the team through the process especially in tough times. A prerequisite -- an ability to translate insights into action. This may require two people to tag-team: a thinker and a doer.
- <u>Copy-Writer</u>: Writing clearly and persuasively is essential here, but also s/he must be skillful at stylizing product Messaging for press releases, social media posts, and message tracks for your Story-Tellers. They must make them live and breathe. This resource will also have a role to play in ensuring all Messaging is cohesive across all of the Engagement Points.

The Core Team is responsible for choosing and assembling an Execution Team comprised of experts with skills and experiences required for successful activation. You may find some skills scale across your Brand-Love vehicles justifying a full-time resource. Other skills may be needed only at certain times necessitating more in-and-out short-timers. In this situation, you will want to source freelancers and specialized agencies that can flex their staffing to accommodate you part-time. Here are the experts whose skills are most essential for your Brand-Love vehicles:

- Social Media Community Manager: Develops and executes the strategy for the brand's social channels and engages with customers on those channels. In addition, s/he will be highly involved in ensuring ALL social content across ALL the channels consistently reinforces the brand's image according to the style guide and your narrative. This expert is on-top and adept of the latest social trends and is able to pro-actively leverage them to drive the Brand-Love vehicles.

- Influencer Marketers: Skilled at identifying and briefing influencer Story-Tellers who can effectively convey the Message. Some Influencer Marketers may be more experienced with social-based influencers (e.g. instagrammers, YouTubers, bloggers, etc.) while others are more public relations (PR) practitioners. The latter will focus on pitching and securing editorial coverage (e.g. print and digital publications, broadcast, etc.).

- Content Creators: These resources are likely external to your organization and include production companies and creative agencies that create content for media (e.g. TV, digital, social, film, print, etc.).

- Experiential Executers: For any events, activations, or experiences, you will want experts who know how to put on a party and get the RIGHT people there. They are responsible for organizing, hiring the right sub-contractors/vendors and executing according to your vision.

- Professional Experts: This can include Lawyers (Intellectual Property, Contract, Trademark, etc.), Accountants, Grant Writers (i.e. if you are seeking funding), and Sales Associates.

Depending on your Brand-Love strategy, a handful of other experts may be needed such as media planners, ecommerce experts, tech builders (e.g. apps, websites/landing pages) just to name a few. Again, these resources will likely fill short-term needs and will flow in and out as required.

By now you are thinking, "This is great and all, but where do I find these people?" And I say, "Leverage your network". For example:

- LinkedIn: Post the talents you are seeking and ask for recommendations.
- Professional: Look within industry organizations, forums and groups.
- Your investors: This is likely not their first rodeo. They have connections to offer.
- Fellow entrepreneurs: Whom have they used? And just as useful, whom do they suggest you avoid?
- The ghosts: Or, the people behind the work you admire. They aren't always easy to identify because as a rule brands don't openly disclose these geniuses. So, you may have to look harder by scouring the accolades celebrating the work like awards and industry media write-ups (e.g. AdAge, Ad-Week, and PRWeek). Also, look at the fine print of press releases. The contacts are generally profiled at the bottom.

- <u>Start-Up Accelerator/Incubator programs:</u> They will have a plethora of resources who can help you with anything you need. Generally these services are offered at a reduced rate or even pro-bono.

And when all else fails, Google search. Just remember to do the proper due-diligence.

So, now you have your infrastructure. There is only one thing left...

CHAPTER 6

CHALLENGES YOU WILL FACE AND HOW TO PERSEVERE

There will be times when the going gets tough that you will want to give up. Your dreams are going to feel like they will never come to fruition. Notice I didn't say "if". You WILL have traffic jams. Your Brand-Love vehicles WILL stall or crash. This is not defeat. It is a call to pause and analyze. Ups and downs are all part of the journey. Here are 5 likely road-blocks and strategies for getting through them:

- At some point (or at many points) you are going to be tempted to just exit onto someone else's successful Super-Highway because that seems easier. Remember, building Brand-Love is hard because YOU have to build it. It doesn't exist because at its essence, **Brand-Love is rooted in an emotional connection to your customer that only YOU can provide**. So, YOU can't follow someone else's map and reach YOUR Brand-Love potential. The best you can do if you opt out is equal your competition which inherently turns you into a commodity.

- You are going to feel overwhelmed and unable to make choices or take action on the decisions in which you have lost confidence. In these situations, return to your "What if..." ideation process and reground yourself in the "what must be true" exercise. This is your home-base if you feel yourself losing focus and starting to waiver. If it is more of a macro concern (i.e. investment, time, risk, etc.), revisit the strategies in Chapter 4 in building Brand-Love on a start-up budget. **Then do something...even if it is small...to move your business forward.** Sometimes it is the small actions that unlock the bigger opportunities hiding in the shadows.

- You are going to be tempted to generalize so you don't alien-ate any potential customers. Let me reiterate that this is the surest way of getting you jammed up on "Interstate Com-modity" where big budgets with a lot of resources are the only way to survive. If your target customer pool is too small and you need broader reach, identify a new target customer and go through the "What if..." Ideation again.

- Not everything is going to go as planned. Even well-con-ceived Brand-Love vehicles can end-up being lemons be-cause you can't control extenuating circumstances...talent can go rogue, journalists delay your story due to breaking news, torrential rain keeps people from coming to an event, the list of etceteras is endless. Have a plan for the more ob-vious risks to help mitigate road-blocks and look for viable detours.

- Your impatience will sabotage you. This will likely happen when your expectations conflict with reality (i.e. I expected more revenue by now, I didn't expect it to take this long, etc.). Panic, disappointment or fear will tempt you into a short-cut. **Before you undermine all the work you have put in, call me. If I don't know how to counsel you, I will find someone who can.** If you have a trusted advisor, call him or her. But make sure this person is an expert in Super-Highway construction and has created love-connections you covet.

So, the time has come to wrap up and wish you well on your journey in building your "Super-Highway of Relevancy". May your highway be a strong, enduring conduit to your customers' hearts, minds and souls. May your Brand-Love vehicles be efficient and expedient in forging love-connections. And may you become a beloved brand where people choose you more often, indefinitely. Let's do this together. Let's make some love!

ENDNOTES

1. According to the Small Business Association (SBA) as cited in: https://www.investopedia.com/slide-show/top-6-reasons-new-businesses-fail/

2. According to Harvard professor Gerald Zaltman as cited in: https://www.inc.com/logan-chierotti/harvard-professor-says-95-of-purchasing-decisions-are-subconscious.html

3. https://www.mondelezinternational.com/en/~/media/MondelezCorporate/Uploads/downloads/OREO_Fact_Sheet.pdf

4. https://secondmeasure.com/datapoints/airbnb-sales-surpass-most-hotel-brands/

5. https://fashionista.com/2015/12/the-laundress

6. https://www.fastcompany.com/90298157/exclusive-laundress-founders-gwen-whiting-and-lindsey-boyd-on-why-they-sold-to-unilever

7. https://www.americanexpress.com/en-us/business/trends-and-insights/articles/cleaning-up-how-a-fabric-care-company-found-success/

8. https://www.fastcompany.com/90298157/exclusive-laundress-founders-gwen-whiting-and-lindsey-boyd-on-why-they-sold-to-unilever

ABOUT THE AUTHOR

Anne Marie Candido is the founder of Go for 2, a Brand "Love" Building consultancy aimed at developing unexpected yet authentic connections to people's heart, mind and soul that will help more people hopelessly fall in love with your brand.

A 20+ year veteran of Procter & Gamble, Anne has been a thought-leader and architect in quickly putting brands on the "Super-Highway of Relevancy" by cultivating Brand-Love. Splitting her decades between Product Development and Communications/ Influencer Marketing, her prevue is unique in that she has been intimately involved in all stages of the brand journey. From game-changing product launches like Secret Clinical Strength as well as pivotal programs like the London 2012 Olympic "Thank You, Mom" campaign and the Cannes award winning Tide Super Bowl Campaigns #BradshawStain and #TideAd, she developed fine-tuned processes to help brands dig deep to discover their Brand-Love potential.

Through partnerships with properties like the NFL, Joe Gibbs Racing, United States Olympic Committee, and NYC Fashion Week, Anne has become an expert in defining how brands can maximize influencers, spokespeople, thought-leaders and credentialers to create relevancy, differentiation and ambassadorship. This expertise has also translated into effective use of social sustainability as evidenced by her leadership of the "Tide Loads of Hope" program. Her work has resulted in billions of high-impact impressions internationally, nationally and locally, across all influencer verticals and channels including: *Ellen, Today, GMA, WSJ, NYT, People, Huffington Post, Popsugar, SI, ESPN* and *BabyCenter* just to name a few.

It was during this time she realized Brand-Love is truly the universal thread that transforms products into brands and brands into franchises. What's more, it didn't matter if the business was small or large, with economical start-up budgets or big budgets, with resources of just a few people to mega-teams...the truth was the same. Brands that intentionally cultivated Brand-Love were the ones who persevered. Armed with this insight and her fine-tuned process principles which she coined *"What If..." Ideation*, she left P&G to embark on a new journey of helping <u>ALL</u> businesses make Brand-Love connections. Her clients range from musicians and makers, to creative and tech agencies, to start-ups and small businesses. All will tell you it isn't easy to cultivate Brand-Love, but it is definitely worth it!

Anne resides in Cincinnati, Oh, with her husband, Tony, and their blended family of 4 "adults in-training". She graduated from the University of Dayton (1998) with a BS in Mechanical Engineering. But don't let that fool you because she is proof you can effectively use both sides of your brain. Anne believes in the power of being connected in mind, body and spirit and that grit is the secret to success.

PS: If you Google her, look under "Anne Westbrook, P&G" too.

www.ingramcontent.com/pod-product-compliance
Lightning Source LLC
Chambersburg PA
CBHW071046220526
45467CB00004B/1694